Show Your Voice

Show Your Voice

초판 1쇄 발행 2024년 8월 16일

지은이 이준원
펴낸이 장길수
펴낸곳 지식과감성#
출판등록 제2012-000081호

교정 주경민
디자인 강샛별
편집 강샛별
검수 이주연, 이현
마케팅 김윤길, 정은혜

주소 서울시 금천구 빛꽃로298 대륭포스트타워6차 1212호
전화 070-4651-3730~4
팩스 070-4325-7006
이메일 ksbookup@naver.com
홈페이지 www.knsbookup.com

ISBN 979-11-392-2066-7(03840)
값 12,000원

- 이 책의 판권은 지은이에게 있습니다.
- 이 책 내용의 전부 또는 일부를 재사용하려면 반드시 지은이의 서면 동의를 받아야 합니다.
- 잘못된 책은 구입하신 곳에서 바꾸어 드립니다.

지식과감성#
홈페이지 바로가기

Show Your Voice

Written by **JoonWon Lee**

Table of Contents

Unread (acknowledgement)	6
What was	8
Mosaic	10
Lost in Translation	11
Seasons of Humanity	14
Perfection	16
Perfection 2	17
World of Imagined Realities	18
Pride	19
Other side	20
Mask	21
Lost	22
Wall	23
Safe	24
Worry	25
Abyss	26
Abuse	27
Enough or Not Enough	28
Survival of the Fittest	29

Niche of Time	30
Of What Once Was	31
Apocalypse	32
Climate Heroes in Action	33
A Chance for Life	35
Moon	37
Write the World	38
Enigma	40
Mountain	41
Loneliness	42
Loneliness 2	43
Serenity	44
Mine	45
Street Signs	46
Jealousy	47
Why vote	49
Poverty	51
Show your voice	52

Unread (acknowledgement)

A book

Its spine uncreased

Its pages crisp

Untouched by curious fingers

Yet to be pried open by the ambitious

A story bound by the silence of neglect

A book

Always opened

Yet never read

Paused in its potential

A world uncharted

Waiting for a breath of life

A book

Its cover worn down

By eyes of fleeting interest

Title traced by indifference

Drawn in ink that has yet

To flow into the invisible lines

A book

A silent plea

My story

Awaits a reader

To navigate the stanzas of possibility

To discover the unwritten meaning within

What was

The gentle breeze starts
The rhythm of the dance of petals
Announcing the fleeting embrace
As the world falls asleep

The fragrance of rain
Quenching nature's thirst
Revitalizing showers
Restore the youth of my home

Fading footprints
As earth becomes anew
Secrets gently revealed
As flaws wash away

A happenstance held close
Memories held tenderly
In the small moments
A grand display unveiled on tapestry

Yet in the quiet spaces
A subtle change
An empty shell replaces
The home once filled with love

Harsh breezes
Bland rain
Secrets mute
Barren earth

Imprinted footprints
Absence of moments
Emotionless memories
A torn tapestry reflects

What was

Mosaic

Beneath my skin's disguise
Lies a puzzle of truths
Broken pieces of
Unfinished projects
Abandoned ideas
Stitched with threads of memory
With silent seams speaking tales
A spirit chasing shadows of who I wish to be
Deluded a mirror and blurred my reflection
A hazed line of reality and fiction
Tracing the shape of being to find identity
Through the labyrinth of self
In the quiet chamber of my soul
I sit weaving
The essence of my existence

Lost in Translation

I live in between two worlds
Both desperately pulling
Trying to win over each other
Alluring me with treasure
Interpretations
Logic

I am a mediator
Navigating through constant strife
Of Java and Python
Arguing over who is superior
"My code is user-friendly" reasons Python
"My code is simpler" counters Java

Simple is better than complex
Special cases aren't special enough to break rules
In the face of ambiguity, I refuse the temptation to guess

Presenting the world as a random collection

Of unrecognized words

Symbols, objects, classes

As I decipher

The layered ingenuity

The hidden message

The hypnotic patterns

I translate the garbled reality

Into the saga of the lost treasure

I sit connecting

Reasonings

Between languages

Between worlds

Of a being

Who conjures one's imagination

I stand behind

The cover of a mediator

I manipulate words

I solve algorithms

I am a confused decoder

Trying to keep the harmony

Between two worlds

Seasons of Humanity

Spring came

A subtle spark

Conjured otherworldly fire

Tales of titans and gods

Engulfing the mind

Binding the present for the future

Infinitely-dimensional possibilities

Summer came

Stonework replaced by

The forging of steel

Hammering power and control

To achieve efficiency

Pouring knowledge into prescriptions

To reach immortality

Fall came

The pinnacle of man

Technology reach heights

Higher than the planes

That pierce the sky

Traversing stars and

Bringing dreams to reality

Winter came

Burnt to ashes by our own fire

Digging graves with stone once more

An idea that a creation surpassed the creator

Conquered by intelligence we considered

Artificial

The seasons reset

So does mankind.

Perfection

So unforgiving
Like a law written in stone but
So beautifully broken
By the glares demanding harmony
The shards of my fragile heart
Have been washed away and lost
In the infertile dooms of oblivion
Only time will tell
The shape of my path
Winding and meandering
Into imperfection

Perfection 2

Perfection is a flaw

For the imperfect

Just another soul

Adding onto the mountain

Of blemishes and failures

Hidden under the shadow of fragile vanity

As the flaw that approves identity

And the mistake that enjoys insecurity

Born to be real not perfect

But I cower under

Fake harmony

And plastic truths

Into the land of the forbidden

A foot soldier of my own fate

Led by the forgotten glory

Shrouded in abnormality

Marching onto

A chasm of dreams and

Flawless imperfections

World of Imagined Realities

Words of absolute ruling

An endless world for a restless mind

From the depths of algorithms

To the layered perfection of logic and syntax

Passion blazes a path

In this pixelated dream

I search for

The hidden key

In the never-ending lines of code

Pride

The weeds of growth
Planted in the garden of my vanity
Choking off my sanity
Thrive in all climates
A nagging thought
That intrudes the soul
I am superior
I alone fly against the wind
Boosted with pride
Of being the best alone
But
With weights of isolation
I alone fly against the wind

Other side

The calm, cool river

Asked me to be embraced

Stars reflect off

The face of the water

Drawn into the journey

To true peace

Showing glimpses

Of life without struggle

A lone oasis

In a dessert of failures

Golden sunsets and immeasurable blues

Dance and harmonize

Through my oceans and lands

A timeless healing

As I reach and grasp

For the other side

Mask

I sit

Facing the wall in front

Facades are hung

For me to choose

Happiness to smile and laugh

Joy to bond and love

Yet I am a paper-thin lie

A shadow

Of who I wish to be

Lost

Between the borders
Of black and white
Confusion led to
The world in grey
I'm never wrong
But do I possess
What I seek?
Have I turned left
Or found right?
My image
Painted on
And resculpted
Until I am
A little of nothing
Lost on a stained canvas
Holding a maze
Of words, ideals, and memories
That was never finished

Wall

I hear screams
Of forgotten memories
What have I left behind?
Reason and sanity
I sit listening
My ear pressed to hear
A deafening silence
As I make out the words
Of the mistaken happiness
Behind that wall

Safe

Am I safe

From the weak and mistaken?

The outcasts that I used to recognize

The once fulfilled world

Slowly seeps through

The holes in my soul

Until I'm empty

Worry

Like a parasite

That feeds on deformed knowledge

Seads of fear planted

In incomplete ideals

Rotting the delicate bond

Between mind and heart

A twisted pain

Induced by the greed

To be perfect

Abyss

Phantasmal realms are seen
Immersed in pain
Intoxicated with pleasure
Beyond the mortal heart
Lies the illusion of escaping
Defy death
Reject logic
Infinite options
Paths open for me
One step forward
To fall in the dark abyss
That welcomes me home

Abuse

My mind is a book

Skimmed through

But not appreciated

Collected then

Thrown and stepped on

Sitting in dust and forgotten

Enough or Not Enough

In a lush life

Options lurk at each turn

Satisfaction a foreign concept

Forever is not enough

Happiness is granted

I want cornucopia

Where curiosity is infinite

Knowledge has no limits

Hunger of mind is unknown

But

Beware

Too much can

Clutter my heart

Cloud my judgement

That will end up owning me

Waiting to realize

That less is more

Fortune makes a fool of me

No higher purpose

Abundance is a blessing and a curse

Survival of the Fittest

In a world that falls apart

Ravenous change

Chugs on my naivety

Gnawing on my reality

How do I outrun?

Surviving is accepting

Living is embracing

Thriving is adapting

Open minds stand on top

Of the rigid shadow looming over me

Niche of Time

A fading world

Sharpens my imagination

A sleepless night

That I own

Where the harmony

Of a choir of caves

And orchestrated trees

Cladded the moon

In the dress stitched with diamond stars

Clouds part like torn curtains

To reveal an unending dream

Accompanied by the lies of silence

The suppressed cries of loss

Give away to the beauty of tomorrow

Of What Once Was

The abandoned are grey
Whether made of bricks, lies, or mistakes
Masking remnants of laughter
Echoing dead conversations
Washing away passion
Along with the desire to be desired
Souls extinguish
Dreams fade
Revealing the skeleton
Of what once was color

Apocalypse

In a better alternate reality

Called the past

I swim against the current of time

Escaping the ravenous grip of tomorrow

Climate Heroes in Action

I was losing

Kicking plastic bottles and caps

Scoring into a trash can

Yet I lose to human greed

In the small imprinted cycle of bottle caps

Behind the Wonderland of lies

Fooling Alice with a white rabbit of pollution

Empty promises driven by the hunger for profit

Leading down into a veil of efficiency

To spend centuries degrading

On the Islands of trash

Marked by the glistening evils of plastics

Brandishing weapons of ruin and destruction

From the grave of failed promises rises

We, the young ones

Are the lone heroes

With heart and grit

Infinite circles tattooed on the soul

Pledging the vows to carry out the vision

Of evergreen tomorrows

Showing scars of shouldering the weight

Of forgotten promises

A Chance for Life

The everchanging time
Studded with the ocean of stories
In the place we call home
The land of struggles
Now scorched under our torch

Broken promises
Charred history
Crumpled dreams
Invade this sanctuary
Flux of wealth and power

The unseen stars
The uncertain ocean floors
The unwilling forest trees
The raging light of fire
Waves of destruction

Admits this tattered world
A lone hero
Armed with heart and grit
Faced with hurt and guilt
Rids the scars of greed

A chance for life
A time for redemption
A path for rebirth
To carry out the will
Of what once was envisioned

Moon

Desperately searching through clouds of emotions
Revolving around a planet of heartbreak
Never show my full heart
Or create craters of rejection
Embraced only by the silence of night
The stars of memories
And the moonlight of longing
Tell secrets
No one believes

Write the World

I am a color-blind artist
Who sees with words and talks in shades
On the black and white canvas
I whisper
A drop of innocence
A splash of knowledge
A streak of harmony
Layered in anew-ed curiosity
To create a world of words
Which I fill with mysteries
In the heart of the story
I search for the light of truth
Lost in a maze of lies
Where each path hisses and glares
Sneering at my ideals
Cornering me into a mold of conformity
Only when I break free
From the binds of standards

And the fog of judgement

I may ascend and rejoice

Donned by the crown of my written world

Enigma

It is a trap of illusion
For moments of pleasure
I give up all I have
Two hearts belong to neither
A phrase that has lost its meaning
"I love you."
What is love?

Mountain

The frozen feet, the light air, a final step, and I stand on top
The struggles of the path I took, was it a futile journey with no end?
Looking down upon the glory of the summit, why do I feel so unfulfilled?

Loneliness

I eat dinner as four seats are filled
Staring into fear, abandonment, and rejection
Who stare back with glass, lifeless eyes
The view of my wall with flickering shadows
Animated with memories that never
happened

Loneliness 2

The cold drops of night
Run down my back
The aching hole in my heart
Missing the man who left
Who goes by the name of solitude
The fake warmth from a blanket
The forced comfort of my house
Awaiting the fraud of happiness
A bed too big for one
As I replicate the joy of company
I left my happiness behind for
The deception of pleasure
The short-lived bliss of hopes and dreams
Crushed by the shadow of loneliness

Serenity

On a circular table

I sit watching

The flickering screams of a candle

Which dance with the wind

The calm of the night

The show of the stars

My memories provide warmth

A lone singularity

In the midst of all companionships

As I embrace the reflection of myself

But I am not abandoned

A gentle absence

That cools the fevered mind

I have no fear

Mine

The feeble promise

Called your word

Does not please my hunger

I am insatiable

I want success

I twist my fate

With the touch of Midas

I will create a world

With a ravenous pride

That consumes my soul

The desire of adding

Prizes like corpses

I offer my life

To my greedy conscience

With gold or lies

To empty is to fill

Street Signs

Turn

Stop

Yield

A simple walk

But I am lost

Flashing lights of life

Announces the coming

Of tomorrow

A reality of no direction

Yet street signs hold firm

A crossroad of fate

As I stumble to my identity

The blurry black letters

On the yellow signs

Lead me home

Jealousy

Eating away my soul

Chipping away my pride

A futile attempt to ignore

The toxic whisper of vanity

The iron grip of insecurity

My heart torn in broken chambers

Filled with anguish poisoning me

The lust of success blinding me

As I head to

The butcher who patiently awaits

Collecting lives like a farmer who harvests

I face the sugar-coated lies of ill wills

On the path for perfection studded by

The envy for those who above

The tears of those beneath

The hate for those on the same fate

The need to be noticed

To turn heads

To be recognized
Hurting others for my insatiable hunger
Whether it be called
Anger, greed, or desire
Sitting on the throne of failures
I plead
The golden wish with a hidden black heart

Why vote

They say I am
Too dark to have a voice
Too frail to defend my country
Too unique to stand up for the majority
Too feminine to rule the world
So
They muzzled me with unanimity
They caged me in uniformity
They hid me in anonymity
They trapped me in inequality

But
As a citizen of this great country
I will not silence my voice
I will not abandon my duty
I will not shy away from my pride
I will not throw away my right
On a sacred mission

To heal the wounds of bad decisions

The scars of old mistakes and

To mend the broken promises

The jagged cracks of society

I will vote

Poverty

In a world of abundance

A land of poverty

Where people thrive off of gluttony

A competition of survival

Plagues the poor

From dawn to dawn

The shadow of loss

Takes the peace

Draining hope and faith

An infectious disease

Under a name of hunger

Hunger for power

Hunger for success

Hunger for escape

A silent thief

Stealing our will

Cutting it down

Only leaving behind

The form, shape, and shadows

Of who we were

Show your voice

The cold bullet of judgment
Numbs me
The wound of past mistakes
Mocks me
The scar of bad decisions
Shames me
The fear of embarrassment
Blinds me
A muffle shrouded in pain
Silences me
I laugh but my heart's locked
I talk but my tongue's tied
I scream but I'm not heard
I lost my voice
I lost myself

I am tied down to my flaws
A strike of reality hits

To break open the ice around my heart
Wake up and recall
I was born with a pride
A confidence to speak
A freedom to express
A road to independence
So
Regain control
Reclaim dignity
Spark the light of pride
Sing a song with passion
Show them
That you have a voice
The you found yourself
That you can be you

Once more.

Closing Poem
Remembrance

There is a bubble

That blocks my thoughts and

Boxes in my ideas

Each step

Contorts the feeble grasps of reality

But every story pops

The layers that fog my mind

Leaving blank space

With nothing to fill in

February, 2024

DoWon Lee

Misinformation

It wasn't me
It was my hands
That spewed
The vile of hatred
That corrodes souls
Into ashes

It wasn't me
It was the vase
That sent
Another breath to the ground
Sparks another lie
Leaving humanity in ruins

Violence

I am stuck in

A vicious cycle

Through my eyes

I see robbery

Through my ears

I hear gunshots

Through my nose

I smell smoke

In this life

We are all

Watered with greed

Fed with fear

And stained with pain

These weeds create

A gaping hole

Where violence resides

Reason

I turn a blind eye
To the horrors unfolding
I live in a place
Where thoughts are muzzled
And lured into pits of cliché
I see the sins
Matching pedants with bigots
That gave birth to lunacy
I will never be sane
In a world
Void of reason

Time

As the silent life streams away
As the heart stops its grand drumming
The chains wrap and drag it underground
Nothing is left behind
No comfort
No love
No joy
But
Time turns still
The sorrow-filled river reaches the heart
In the hourglass of need
With tears to feed your soul

Gluttony

Grab and take

And get robbed double

You are a thief sacked by Lupin

Steal and horde

And find yourself empty

You are sitting on a landfill of dreams

Have the universe

But never feel satisfied

You will choke on the weeds of greed

Pride has left the tatters of my soul

Carried away in the whispers of prejudice

But I will not water the vile of hate

I have found my courage hiding in the

shadows

And sparked my hope from the faded burns

I am not afraid

I can speak now

I can show my voice now

I have found the exit

Show Your Voice

Hearts are shattered from the gashes of fear
The cries of help are met with scorn
I want to shout what I've been through
But I seal my mouth and run back home
Trapped by these monsters who taunt the weak
And silence their thoughts
I want my justice but none is given
I am stranded
Left in rags

Turning away
Running away
I see the tyrants ready to pounce
The hatred from their words
Burns my soul and strips my pride
Screams of crimson tears scar my barren heart
Leaving nothing but pain and shame
What am I?
Just a coward unable to help himself

Colored or Not?

Shine in vivid images
Where anger is red
A fire that burns with rage
While blue is the serenity
That calms the weary mind
Trees are splatches
Of green and brown
While the sun is a burst
Of yellow blazing the Earth
A life of color
A life of imagination
But I can't see
I only see black and white
A white sun
A gray sky
And black clouds
I only feel pain
My life is dull
In shades of black

Free

I can't breathe
The cold blinding my path
I can't scream
The depth silencing my voice
I drag myself out
But the tide taunts me
Hooks lure me into the open air
I attempt my final escape
Thrashing and twisting
Snapping and biting
Roasted on a fire

But dims when needed the most?

Why must I listen

Who corrupts to get his ways

And taints the soul of the pure

So

Walk with me

Pave a new path

In this fight for democracy

Where we cut down

The forests of tyranny and fear

And plant the seeds

Of freedom and joy

Catch the light

That glazes away night

To forge a world

Where democracy shines

What democracy means to me

I live in a world where
Injustice thrives
Inequality looms
Hopes shatter
Thoughts blur
Reality taunts my dream

Dragging me down
To a chasm of nightmare
The future seems bleak
Freedom feels far away
Is it even there?

Why must I live
Where one rules over
And silences those who stand up?
Why must I cower
While light seems so close

Reality 2

Death is inevitable
Yet here I am
Stuck in a vast desert
Where souls turn into sand
And the wind is their screams
The mirage taunts me
Blocking my way to salvation
Blocking my way to reality
Of life

Reality

Time has left him
But he starts his journey for oblivion
Trudging his way
Losing all reality
Of the man he once was

Rebuilding the Door of
my Reality

Align

Preordained by God

Or sent in coincidence?

Conscience in decision

Or a whim of the winds?

Haunted by the unknown

Blown away into a maze

Where every entrance meets no exit

Now left behind

In the shadows of the web

That leaves nothing but tremors

In the path of fate

Misery

Waking up

Like a marionette without a puppeteer

Craving for what you can't have

Hope turns into a sorrow

From the pain life brings

When a moment snaps

Misery reigns in tide

A circle of isolation

With none stopping its path

Vertigo

I look down

To see the adventure that awaits me

Trip and fall

But feel the air start to rush by

Exhilaration coursing through my veins

And race into the stars

But as the moon trembles

And the stars shake

I

Fall

To the jagged land

I can't defy vertigo

Shattered

From the deep and hollow

The waves of a nightmare

Course through the stormy heart

Huddled on a raft

That struggles for its survival

Lays a cracked vase

Seeping out its hope

Out into the sea

That haunts my shattered mind

Truth

You wake up to find
That you are all alone
In a dark pit
With nowhere left to hide
You feel the ashes rising
Choking and pinning you down
Under the gray hills of mendacity
Trying to tell the truth
But no words escape
Futile attempts to scream
To tell them to stop
But silence is heard
And the truth is buried
So is my conscience

Insatiable

Stand and wait

For the world to disappear

Within the dark

Hear the song tuned with sorrow

And strung with tears

The notes ring off the walls

Each echo

Humming a melody of silence

Whispering a secret of solitude

Feeding a chasm of greed

Called a void

Dulled

Do I have freedom?

Or a mere image framed by greed

Is there a place to go?

In a struggle to stake claim

Dumped in the scarred paradise

With life edged away

Into a speck of dust

I can't stop these monsters

Incased with vain glory

Chasing fame and riches

But as they beg for a change in their lives

They wither away before my eyes

Leaving my world

All

Gray

Age

Through the windows

And pass the doors

To find the clock that measures

Every breath

Some flash in seconds

Others drone on

But after the clock rings

The souls travel

Into my grasp

Where they are

My own

Desert

Where time is gauged
By the sighs of the wind
Each day takes
A grain of my sanity
In the fields of void
Where in its midst
Holds an hourglass
Shifting with no trace of change
Inside nature's arid breath
Carrying away those in the night
Plunging them into
The seas of sand

Agony reigns in the contorted mirrors

Lurking behind the horizon

Inside the dome of horror

Where time is a shadow of reminiscence

That never seems to catch up

To the world that I live in

Realities obscure into vivid dreams

Changing the truth and mixing with lies

A trap my imagination has held

That is alone and somber

Where I am

Always

Broken

Broken

Thrown out
And stranded on the streets of anonymity
Lost in the crosswalks of shame and regret
Is a wish for a better tomorrow
That whispers empty promises
Trapping my mind in the cycle of terror
Withering the garden of dreams
Planting thorns that slowly devour
The roots of prosperity and imagination
That once anchored my pride and aspiration
But now holds an empty vase of hope
Shattered and blown from the winds of self-doubt
Leaving a dulled blade that serves no purpose
Left to tarnish and rust in the wind
In the city that always sleeps
The lights never turn on but flicker with shame
But without a daylight blinding shards of
despair

Those who Crush
the Doors
of my
Imagination

Nightmare

Drift away into a story

Guarded with fear

And built off distrust

Enter the world connected with hatred

With scarred memories in its midst

I cower in fear

A twist and turn

I try to escape this haunted time

A nightmare of life

But each step
Lights up a new road
With new risks
And a new life

Step

I'm trapped

In a mental game

I am overwhelmed

Taking a step

Into the unknown

And escape the maze

That keeps me painting

The same picture

Walking the same trail

But

Take a journey

Into a new life

Where courage fills

The cracks in the road

Where dreams hold together

On this marathon

I may wander off the maze

And walk away from the path

Bonds of Colors 2

Strands of silk

Fibers of wool

Threads of cotton

Meet with acids to begin

Its lively march

Awaken by the spectra

A covalent bond forms

Strong and firm

Vivid with color

Just like us

Bonds of Colors

I've always been taught

That the sun is yellow

The sea is blue

Grass is green

And that space is black

But what if

The sun is orange

The sea is purple

Grass is yellow

And that space is white

Life is a mixture of colors

I am dancing on the thread of races

In this trance

I sing a song of tomorrow

I walk along the banks of promise

And I dance to the rhythm of justice

Freeing myself from the chains

That brought pain and grief

To keep living for a new journey

To the hope of the future

Let's dream together

On the treasure island of time

Each turn is clear with a path

With hope for the next life

The next world

The next sunrise

That marks the start

Of a new day full

Into the world of hope

I Am Hopeful Because

I was trapped in the reign of terror
That scared hope to flutter away
Flapping against the winds of prejudice and
hate
Struggling to stay afloat
Above the lands of denial
Soaked by a river of fire
Scorched by judgement and inequality

But in the moment of despair
When the sky washes over
Through patience and tears
Turning barren to fertile
A seed of restoration will bloom
Calming the winds into a whisper
But am I truly free?

Imagination

A realm of curiosity

In a world of the impossible

Where my thoughts

Spring with life

And where my dreams

Dance in harmony

Flows of red and gold

Swirl and churn into a crimson door

That guards me from

The fetter of truth

If opened

Reality disappears

I am lost in

The maze of my imagination

Space

Hold me up high
So I can dance with the stars

Bring me a starry night
So I can talk to the moon

Until then
I dream my hopes into reality
And walk along the star of miracles

I open my eyes and stare
Into the untouched beauty
Of a dream

Dream

Closing my eyes in anticipation

For the events of a lifetime

I step into a box

That shifts when I walk

And creates what I imagine

Lost in the hazy boundaries

Between

What's real and

What's not

I see a crimson door

That opens into

The land of possibilities

I dash towards

The endless ideas

Where I find myself

Drifting into a realm

The colors start to form

A picture that is too fragile

The Bursting Door of
Imagination

Intro Poem
Dreams, Memories, And Reality

I'm at the start line
The first page of my story
The vivid dreams of mine start to take life
Into a tale of hopes

I've been working for this dream
I have nothing to cling onto
Just memories
To color my dull life

Broken and frail
The reality of life shatters my hopes
And leaves me with faded images
Of my dreams and memories

Dulled	30
Insatiable	31
Truth	32
Shattered	33
Vertigo	34
Misery	35
Align	36

Rebuilding the Door of my Reality

Reality	40
Reality 2	41
What democracy means to me	42
Free	44
Colored or Not?	45
Show Your Voice	46
Gluttony	48
Time	49
Reason	50
Violence	51
Misinformation	52

Closing Poem

Remembrance	53

Table of Contents

Acknowledgment   5

Intro Poem
Dreams, Memories, And Reality   9

The Bursting Door of Imagination
Dream   12

Space   14

Imagination   15

I Am Hopeful Because   16

Bonds of Colors   18

Bonds of Colors 2   19

Step   20

Nightmare   22

Those who Crush the Doors of my Imagination
Broken   26

Desert   28

Age   29

Acknowledgment

As I grow
I find ideas I strive to reach
Some are dreams for the future
Or memories from the past
But this poem book is a reality
From my dreams and memories
That are brought to life

June, 2023
DoWon Lee

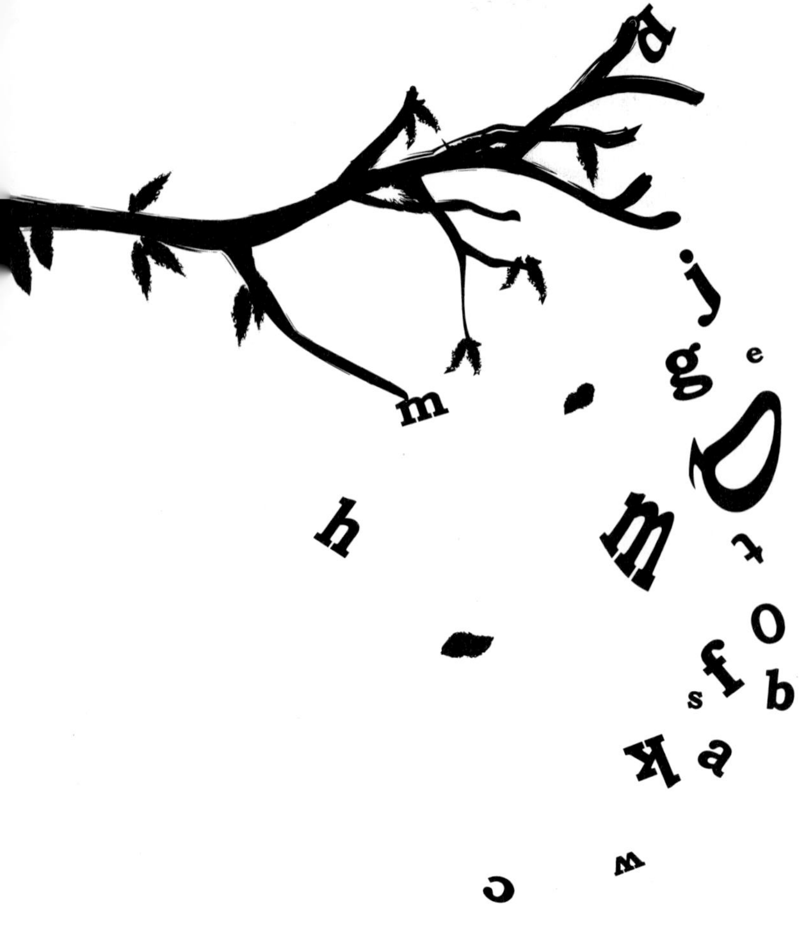

The Door is Open,
You Know

Written by **DoWon Lee**

All proceeds from the sale of this book will be donated to The Nature
Conservancy to help conserve the lands and waters which all life
depends on.

The Door Is Open, You Know

초판 1쇄 발행 2024년 8월 16일

지은이 이도원
펴낸이 장길수
펴낸곳 지식과감성#
출판등록 제2012-000081호

교정 주경민
디자인 강샛별
편집 강샛별
검수 이주연, 이현
마케팅 김윤길, 정은혜

주소 서울시 금천구 벚꽃로298 대륭포스트타워6차 1212호
전화 070-4651-3730~4
팩스 070-4325-7006
이메일 ksbookup@naver.com
홈페이지 www.knsbookup.com

값 12,000원

• 이 책의 판권은 지은이에게 있습니다.
• 이 책 내용의 전부 또는 일부를 재사용하려면 반드시 지은이의 서면 동의를 받아야 합니다.
• 잘못된 책은 구입하신 곳에서 바꾸어 드립니다.

지식과감성#
홈페이지 바로가기

The Door is Open,
You Know